Sally's Sandcastles

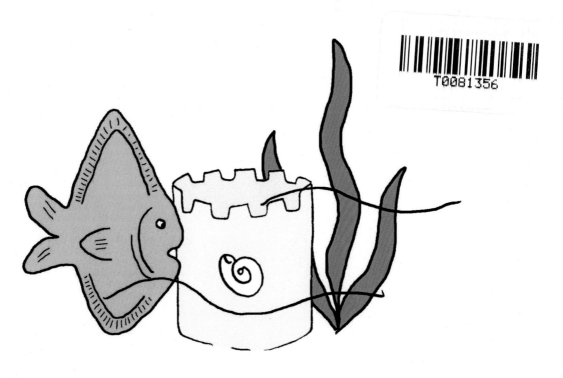

Sally and her Mum were bored sitting around their house.

Sally looked out the window to see the sun was shining.

"It's so sunny outside, we should go to the beach!" said Sally excitedly.

So they drove to the beach and then walked along the **s**and.

Suddenly Sally saw a bucket and spade,
sitting in the sand all by itself.

"Look Mum, I can build some sandcastles!
I'll just go for a swim first," said Sally.

Sally went swimming in the **s**ea and then **s**at down on the **s**and. She de**c**ided to build **s**ome **s**andca**s**tles.

Sally filled her bucket with **s**and, turned it over and put it down with a SPLAT.

Sally slid the bucket off and out came a **s**andca**s**tle.

Sally made more and more, and soon
she was surrounded by a city of sandcastles!

Mum helped Sally cover her
sandcastles with seashells.

Sally and her Mum were hungry, so they drove back to their house for some lunch.

They sat at the table and ate some sandwiches.

"Can we go and visit my **s**andca**s**tles tomorrow?" asked **S**ally.

"Ye**s**, but only if it's **s**unny again," Mum **s**aid.

That afternoon the tide came in
–s-s-s-s-s-s-s-s-s-s-s-s-s-s-s- swoosh!

The **s**ea washed all the **s**andca**s**tles away.

The next day was **s**unny again, **s**o Mum and
Sally went back to the beach. **S**ally looked
and looked for her **s**andca**s**tles
but they had di**s**appeared!

"Where did they go?" asked **S**ally **s**adly.

"I'm **s**orry **S**ally, the tide must have washed them away into the **s**ea," **s**aid Mum.

Sally smiled.

"That's ok. The fish can u**s**e them for hou**s**e**s**! Let's make **s**ome more hou**s**e**s** for the fish!"

So they did.